ORANGES

by ZACK ROGOW · Pictures by MARY SZILAGYI

Orchard Books • A division of Franklin Watts, Inc. • New York and London

Text copyright © 1988 by Zack Rogow   Illustrations copyright © 1988 by Mary Szilagyi

The text for *Oranges,* in different form, first appeared in *A Preview of the Dream* (1985) by Zack Rogow.

Orchard Books, 387 Park Avenue South, New York, New York 10016
Orchard Books Great Britain, 10 Golden Square, London W1R 3AF England
Orchard Books Australia, 14 Mars Road, Lane Cove, New South Wales 2066
Orchard Books Canada, 20 Torbay Road, Markham, Ontario 23P 1G6

Orchard Books is a division of Franklin Watts, Inc.

Manufactured in the United States of America   Book design by Mina Greenstein
The text of this book is set in 20pt. ITC Zapf International Medium. The illustrations are colored pencil and watercolor, reproduced in four-color halftone.
10 9 8 7 6 5 4 3 2 1

Library of Congress Cataloging-in-Publication Data
Rogow, Zack. Oranges / by Zack Rogow: illustrations by Mary Szilagyi.
Summary: Describes the long journey and the
combined labor of many people that it takes to bring a single orange from the tree to the table.   ISBN 0-531-05743-7.   ISBN 0-531-08343-8 (lib. bdg.)
1. Orange—Juvenile literature.
2. Orange industry—Juvenile literature.   [1. Orange.]   I. Szilagyi, Mary. ill.   II. Title.   SB370.O7R64   1988   634'.31—dc 19   87-22884   CIP   AC

To my mother-in-law · Z.R.

To Steve · M.S.

Somebody cleared the fields.
Somebody toppled the pines,
upturned the stumps.

Someone ploughed the rows
straight as sunbeams in the heat.

Probably he spoke Spanish.

Someone stirred a hole for the seed,
cupped soil around the base of a seedling
that sprang back deep green.

Somebody grafted that branch
to the base of a Rough Lemon tree,
bandaged the cut
and watched it heal and blossom.

Someone shoveled the irrigation ditches
and dusted the dirt
with mineral powders.

Then one day someone walked up the tree
and twisted off the oranges,
admiring one that was just about perfect.

Probably she spoke Creole.

Someone heaved the full field boxes
onto the carts behind the tractor,
somebody hauled them to the truck
that hauled them to the plant
where the fruit was poured onto the conveyor.

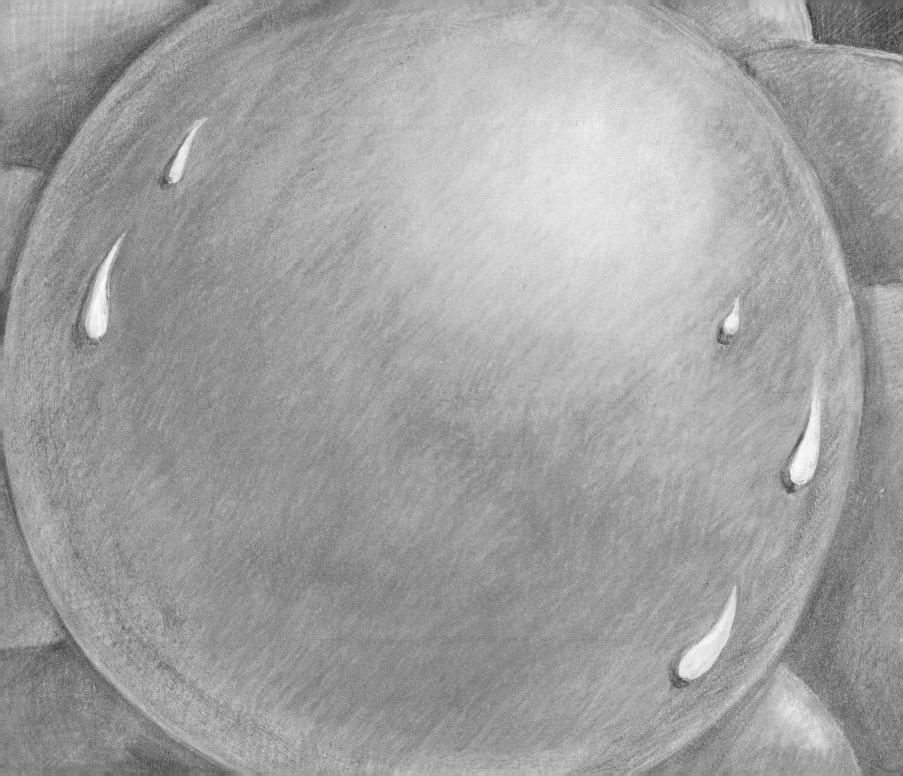

Someone adjusted the gas,
bleaching the green out of the skins.
Some women picked out the speckled ones
that are used to make juice,
and some men sprayed wax on the prettier ones,
branded them with ink.

Then someone assembled the fruit
in corrugated cardboard, slid on the tops,
and banded the boxes to the skids.
Somebody twirled the wheel of the fork lift
that boosted the oranges into a truck.

Some trucker drove them north,
stopping at he forgot what diner
to sniff coffee and hear live voices.

Probably he spoke English.

Later someone selected a crate
and carted it from market to storefront.
Somebody built the pyramids
of fruit at the vegetable stand.

Someone bagged this one
and typed its price on the register.

Probably he spoke Korean.

A world of work
is in this ripe orange that I pry apart.

I place a section
in my mouth
and its liquid fibers
dissolve on my tongue.